EXTINCT

IN THIS SERIES BY BEN GARROD AND GABRIEL UGUETO

Hallucigenia

Dunkleosteus

Trilobite

Lisowicia

Tyrannosaurus rex

Megalodon

Thylacine

Hainan gibbon

ALSO BY BEN GARROD

The Chimpanzee and Me

So You Think You Know About Dinosaurs? series:

Diplodocus

Triceratops

Spinosaurus

Tyrannosaurus rex

Stegosaurus

Velociraptor

EXTINCT
HALLUCIGENIA

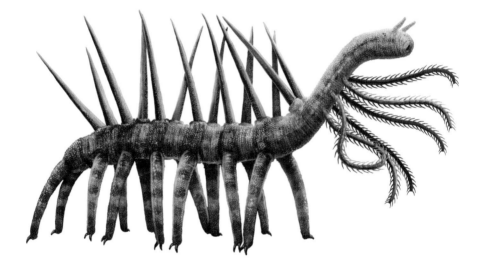

Ben Garrod
Illustrated by Gabriel Ugueto

ZEPHYR
An imprint of Head of Zeus

This is a Zephyr book, first published in the UK in 2021
by Head of Zeus Ltd
This paperback edition first published in the UK in 2022
by Head of Zeus Ltd, part of Bloomsbury Publishing Plc

9 7 5 3 1 2 4 6 8

A catalogue record for this book is available from
the British Library.

ISBN (PB): 9781838935276
ISBN (E): 9781838935283

Typesetting and design
by Catherine Gaffney

Printed and bound in Serbia
by Publikum d.o.o.

Head of Zeus Ltd
5–8 Hardwick Street
London EC1R 4RG
WWW.HEADOFZEUS.COM

'In the end we will conserve only what we love, we will love only what we understand, and we will understand only what we are taught.'

Baba Dioum

CONTENTS

INTRODUCTION

For as long as there has been life on Earth, there has been extinction, and given enough time, all species will one day go extinct. It is too easy to think extinction is terrible and that we should do all we can to stop a species from going extinct. That makes sense, doesn't it? The loss of a species seems an awful and unnatural process, caused by the effects of humans, right?

The concept of extinction is something many of us are familiar with, although, in fact, it's one we might not fully understand. Very often, extinction is a sad, unacceptable and disastrous ending for a species, but from the point of view of a biologist, it is a fundamental part of nature. It is as important to a species as moving, feeding and breeding.

I'm an evolutionary biologist and I've worked with some of the strangest, most beautiful, iconic and heartbreakingly threatened animals on our planet. I understand *how* species go extinct and *why*. But it is still a deeply upsetting event for me when I hear that a species (any species) has gone extinct – or worse, is rapidly being pushed into the history books because of us. We are bombarded by endless news reports about species threatened with extinction, habitats being destroyed and the impacts of global climate change.

I wanted to write this series to explain what's at stake if we carry on as we are. I want to explore extinction as a biological process and investigate why it can sometimes be a positive thing for evolution, as well as, at times, the most destructive force in nature. Let's put it under the microscope and find out everything there is to know about it. Extinction is an incredible process and understanding it enables us to understand the world that little bit better and to make a difference.

When a species is declared extinct, we place a dagger symbol (†) next to its name when it's listed or mentioned in a scientific manner. So, if you do see the name of a species with a little dagger after it, you'll know why. It's extinct.

In this series, I have written about eight fantastic species. Starting with *Hallucigenia* (†), then *Dunkleosteus* (†) and trilobites (†), through to *Lisowicia* (†), *Tyrannosaurus rex* (†) and megalodon (†), before finishing on thylacine (†) and lastly, the Hainan gibbon. Of these, only the Hainan gibbon does not have a dagger next to its scientific name, meaning it is the only one we still have a chance of saving.

Professor Ben Garrod

WHAT IS EXTINCTION?

SPECIES EVOLVE; they change and adapt to their environments and eventually, they go extinct. But don't get me wrong. Just because extinction is natural, it doesn't mean we should sit back and let it happen. Getting burned by the sun is natural, but we still sensibly put on sun lotion to protect ourselves. Each extinction is different, each loss unique, and the truth is that while sometimes we can't do anything to tackle extinction, sometimes we can.

Before investigating when we should try to tackle extinction, we first need to understand it as a natural process. What drives extinction, and what makes some species go extinct more easily than others? When we hear the words 'extinct' or 'extinction', we usually think two things. First, we imagine the dinosaurs, because they're probably the most iconic and familiar group to go through the extinction process. I bet you thought of a *Tyrannosaurus rex*, *Diplodocus* or *Triceratops*, didn't you? Second, we often think that if something has gone extinct then maybe it was a bit rubbish in some way and, possibly, even deserved to disappear.

Well, both ideas are wrong. First, the dinosaurs are most certainly not the only group to have faced extinction, and in fact, as I am sure many of you know, they technically never actually completely died out, but that's a story for another time. And second, as I've already mentioned, going extinct is natural and happens to pretty much every type of animal, plant, fungi, bacteria and other life form that has ever existed or is ever likely to, and has nothing to do with how 'good' or 'bad' a species is.

Even a quick look at extinction shows us how widespread, devastating and yet important it is.

But before we understand all that, what exactly do we mean by the word extinct? We may have a general idea that it's something to do with a species not being 'alive' anymore. Something is extinct when the last individual of that species or group dies and there are absolutely no more to replace it. Because extinction has been present since the first life on Earth popped into existence, this must mean that loads and loads of species have gone extinct. It's hard to get your head around how many species this has happened to already. Scientists predict that as many as 99 per cent of the species that have ever lived have gone extinct and if you're wondering how many species that might actually be, then if their calculations are correct, it means we have already lost an almost unbelievable five billion species from our planet.

It's difficult to be certain because many of these extinctions stretch back millions (or even hundreds of millions) of years and because there wasn't a scientist standing there with a camera or a notebook, we shall never know about many of these species. Even today, scientists believe that there may be 10–14 million different species (although some scientists believe this figure might even be as high as one trillion) but of those, only 1.2 million have been documented and recorded in a proper scientific way, meaning we don't know about 90 per cent of life on planet Earth right now.

Here's where it gets a little complicated. Extinction is natural. Even we human beings will go extinct one day. It might sound sad but that's because you're thinking from the point of view of a person. We are simply one of those 14 million or so species, remember. Usually, a species has about 10 million years or so of evolving, eating, chasing, playing, maybe doing homework, building nests or even going to the moon before it goes extinct and ends up in the history (or even prehistory) books. Some species last longer than this, some are around for less time.

Every single species evolves to be perfectly suited to a particular ecosystem or habitat and acts in a way that will help it survive and have young. We call this its niche. Extinction happens when a species can no longer survive in its niche. Lots of different things can cause this and some are more natural than others. Some kill off one species and others cause the loss of thousands or even millions of species at once, making extinction one of the most complex, interesting and important things to study in science.

When we think about the world in which *Hallucigenia* lived, so much was different – from the predatory animals at the top of the food chain, down to very early communities of sponges.

WHY DO SPECIES GO EXTINCT?

A RECENT report stated that approximately one million (1,000,000) species on Earth are threatened with extinction. This number already sounds unthinkably high, but it only includes animals and plants and not any of the other groups of living organisms essential to the well-being of the planet. If they were included, then the number would be even higher. Much higher.

But why *do* species go extinct? It's not as though human hunters will kill all these species and realistically, climate change can't be responsible for every single loss. As you'll see, there are lots of reasons for extinction, but is there a common link? What makes certain species more likely to go extinct than others? It's an interesting question, which many scientists are investigating.

At its most simple, extinction happens when something bad occurs too quickly in the environment of a species or is too severe for the species to overcome. Imagine if a small population of frogs lived on a tiny island and on that island a volcano erupted, covering the land with lava. If the eruption was sudden and the frogs had nowhere to go... well then, it's bye-bye frogs. But what if the eruption happened more slowly and the frogs had time to escape, maybe some finding a safe, damp rock ledge or a tiny stream that survived the lava flow? It's possible that one or two might survive and the species might just make it. Hurray!

When a species does not have the opportunity to respond to a change in the environment, then it is likely to go extinct. What sort of response from the species do we mean here? Well, it might be a physical change, such as colour or size, or a change in behaviour, such as moving to another habitat or eating something different. It might also be a change so small it's only seen right down in its genes, in the DNA. In terms of what sort of 'changes in the environment' might cause an extinction, these can be either in the physical environment of the species, such as habitat destruction in the forests of Borneo, higher temperatures in the Arctic, or increased acidic conditions on the Great Barrier Reef. Or maybe in its 'biological environment' such as the arrival of a new predator, like cane toads being introduced to Australia. Or the development of a new deadly disease – for example, a virus which might start in bats, jumping to humans and then to great apes in the wild. For each of these changes, the species needs to adapt, or it will die.

Scientists have estimated that the average 'lifespan' of a species is between one million and 10 million years, before it goes extinct. Let's look more closely at the variety of causes that can contribute directly or indirectly to the extinction of a species, or group of species.

DISEASES, PREDATION AND COMPETITION

These can either be naturally occurring, and have been for the last 450 million years, or, as more recently, they can result from human actions.

You might wonder how a disease can be down to humans. But take frogs, for example. Their numbers are plummeting worldwide, largely due to a terrible fungal disease called chytrid (kit-rid). Although we're still not 100 per cent certain, it is possible this was caused when African clawed frogs were transported from southern Africa to the rest of the world a few decades ago, as a means to test for pregnancy in humans.

That sounds weird now, but back then we didn't have modern testing techniques. Instead, we relied on testing whether someone was pregnant or not by taking pee from a woman and seeing if it caused a reaction on the ovary of a frog in a laboratory. Strange, but true! It seems the African clawed frogs aren't affected by the fungus, but when they were taken all around the world for pregnancy testing, they took the lethal chytrid with them, where it affected species with no natural immunity. As a result, over 500 species of frogs, toads, salamanders and other amphibians are in decline because of chytrid, with catastrophic drops of up to 99 per cent in population size in some species.

Predation is another factor, which may or may not be natural. An example where humans are unexpectedly linked to predation is lionfish, which are native to the Indian and Pacific oceans. These colourful, venomous predators were kept as pets in aquaria in the USA, but when they were released, many ended up in the Caribbean, where they caused massive destruction to fish populations on the reefs there.

When it comes to competition, in some cases resources in ecosystems, such as food and shelter, might be limited, causing species to be in direct competition with one another. If a species cannot compete, then it's possible it may be driven into extinction.

COEXTINCTION

Sometimes a species has evolved alongside another species so closely that they become dependent on one another, so when one goes extinct, there is nothing the other can do but go extinct too. For example, a specific

parasite that depends on a specific host species – figs must have a specific little parasitic wasp in order to fruit. Or some pollinating insects need one species of plant in order to survive. Darwin's moth in Madagascar has such a long proboscis, it can only feed from deep, funnel-like orchids.

An extreme example of a coextinction is the moa and the Haast's eagle. Moa were huge flightless birds found in New Zealand. Some were as much as 230kg in weight and 3.6m in height, which is nearly twice as tall as an average ostrich. The Haast's eagle, the largest eagle ever, was their main predator. When human settlers hunted the last moa into extinction about 600 years ago, the eagles were left with no food and they too went extinct.

When the large flightless moa were hunted into extinction on New Zealand's South Island, it also meant the end for the Haast's eagle.

GENETIC MIXING

This isn't pollution in the way you might usually understand it, but every species has a set of genetic data unique to that particular group. It's like the recipe for the species. If a little bit of it is altered, then it becomes a different species, just like when ingredients from one recipe get mixed up with another. When the genetic material for a species is altered by the presence of 'other' genetic material, then we call this 'genetic mixing'. This can happen naturally, as in the case where some species of monkey in Africa living near one another interbreed. Or it can happen because humans are to blame.

One well-known example of this is the Scottish wild cat in (you guessed it) Scotland. These cats are a unique species but are nearly all gone now because house cats are able to breed with them and the babies they have together are a mix between the pet cat you might have at home and the Scottish wild cat. They might not look very different (in fact, they may even look the same) but they're not the same. The species we started with has changed and, eventually, may disappear altogether. When we have two species breeding together like this, we call it hybridisation, and the offspring are called hybrids.

HABITAT DESTRUCTION

It is clear to see how habitat destruction and change is causing extinctions now. We only have to look at the forests being torn down in Indonesia, Malaysia and West Africa to clear land for palm oil production, or the Great Barrier reef where the dumping of chemicals and other waste products is polluting and killing the reef. Habitat destruction has always featured significantly as a cause of extinctions throughout the history of life on Earth. Even the world in which the subject of this book, *Hallucigenia*, evolved, meaning the habitats it needed were lost, leading to the extinction of the species. When habitat change or destruction is an influence for extinction, it might be because that habitat is completely removed, or has been poisoned or its temperature has changed. A whole host of changes to a habitat can bring about an extinction event.

CLIMATE CHANGE

This is one cause of extinctions you will definitely have heard of recently. We saw our first extinction of a mammal caused by human-related climate change in February 2019, when the Bramble Cay melomys (a member of the rodent family found only on an island at the northern tip of the Great Barrier Reef) was declared extinct. With sea level rises causing habitat loss on Bramble Cay, the little rodent species could not survive.

There have been several extinctions throughout the history of Earth, where climate change has had a devastating effect. If you're having problems thinking of an example, then probably the most famous was at the end of the Cretaceous period, 66 million years ago, when the famous 'dinosaur-killing asteroid' struck what is now the sea off northern Mexico and caused immediate and long-lasting climate impacts.

Even as I write, I've read that, for the first time, Antarctica has recorded a temperature above 20° C. What effect will this have on the cold-loving marine invertebrates and the whales that depend on them? And, on a much bigger scale, what global impact will the melting of thousands of millions of tonnes of ice have on sea levels and the future climate of the Earth?

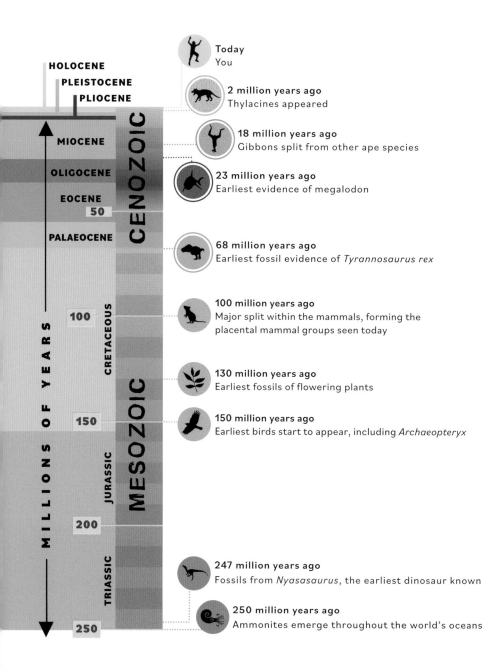

HOLOCENE

PLEISTOCENE

PLIOCENE

Today
You

2 million years ago
Thylacines appeared

MIOCENE

18 million years ago
Gibbons split from other ape species

OLIGOCENE

23 million years ago
Earliest evidence of megalodon

EOCENE

50

PALAEOCENE

68 million years ago
Earliest fossil evidence of *Tyrannosaurus rex*

CENOZOIC

100

CRETACEOUS

100 million years ago
Major split within the mammals, forming the placental mammal groups seen today

130 million years ago
Earliest fossils of flowering plants

150

150 million years ago
Earliest birds start to appear, including *Archaeopteryx*

MESOZOIC

JURASSIC

MILLIONS OF YEARS

200

TRIASSIC

247 million years ago
Fossils from *Nyasasaurus*, the earliest dinosaur known

250 million years ago
Ammonites emerge throughout the world's oceans

250

MILLIONS OF YEARS

PERMIAN

CARBONIFEROUS

DEVONIAN

SILURIAN

ORDOVICIAN

CAMBRIAN

PROTEROZOIC

ARCHEAN

PALAEOZOIC

300

350

400

450

500

300 million years ago
Lisowicia first appeared

320 million years ago
'Mammal-like reptiles', including *Dimetrodon*, evolve

340 million years ago
Earliest amphibians

382 million years ago
Earliest evidence of *Dunkleosteus*

385 million years ago
Oldest fossilised tree

400 million years ago
Earliest fossils of insects

Some of the dates for earliest fossils are estimates based on our best understanding right now. They are not always perfect and the more evidence we collect, the more certain we can be and the more accurate these dates will eventually become.

500 million years ago
Fossil evidence from *Hallucigenia*

520 million years ago
Earliest vertebrates emerged (and may have looked like small eels)

530 million years ago
Earliest fossils of trilobites

680 million years ago
Earliest ancestors of jellyfish and their relatives

2.15 billion years ago
Earliest evidence of bacteria

3 billion years ago
Earliest evidence of viruses

MASS EXTINCTIONS

RIGHT NOW, somewhere in the world, something, for some reason, will be going extinct, hopefully due to natural causes. In the same way that the evolution and appearance of a species is completely natural, so too is the constant loss of species. Species come and go in a constant cycle, a little bit like the tides moving back and forth or the changing of the seasons.

Extinction is unavoidable and goes on at a fairly predictable rate wherever life exists. We call this background extinction: constant, low-level extinction which doesn't really cause major problems on a wider scale – other than for the species going extinct, that is. These 'everyday extinctions' go mostly unnoticed by the majority of us – had *you* heard of the Bramble Cay melomys?

This all changes when we talk about a mass extinction. Mass extinctions, as you might expect, involve loss of life on a huge scale, either across a large number of species or groups, or across a significant part of the planet, or both. In a mass extinction event, the rate of species being lost is greater than the rate by which species are evolving. Imagine filling a bucket with water slowly but there's a big hole in the side of it; over time, the bucket will still become empty. Over the last 500 million years or so, the Earth has experienced multiple mass extinctions, ranging from five to as many as 20 (depending on what definitions (and there are a number of different ones) scientists use). In the worst of these mass extinction events, over 90 per cent of life on Earth has been wiped out, and in terms of life recovering to a level from before the event, it may take at least 10 million years for biodiversity levels to return to what they were. Some mass extinctions, like the one caused by the asteroid 66 million years ago at the end of the Cretaceous period, are pretty quick, while others spread across hundreds of thousands of years to take full effect.

When we talk about mass extinctions, most scientists agree there are five classic mass extinctions, with the earliest occurring around 450 million years ago and the most recent 66 million years ago. In addition to these famous five mass extinctions, another was identified recently, which struck around 2.5 million years ago. Now, many scientists say we are entering (or even in) the sixth mass extinction event, but this is something which needs to be looked at closely for two reasons. First, I've mentioned the recently identified mass extinction which occurred just over two million years ago, which would make that the sixth mass extinction and the current global extinction event would be the seventh, in fact. Second, as we'll see later in the series, it's really hard to say exactly when most mass extinctions start, so, as bad as it is right now, we may not even be in one yet.

Throughout the series, we're going to look at the five classic mass extinctions, the newly discovered mass extinction and the current extinction event which is being triggered by us. Finally, we'll look at how scientists and conservationists are tackling the threat of extinction now and explore what can be done.

THE
END ORDOVICIAN
MASS EXTINCTION

WE START with the first of the best-known five mass extinctions: the End Ordovician (ordo vish-EE-un) mass extinction, which was made up of two different extinctions. These took place roughly one million years apart, with the first event beginning around 443 million years ago.

Said to be the second most devastating mass extinction ever, this claimed 85 per cent of the species living in seas and oceans around the world. It only affected marine ecosystems, because organisms had not really made it onto land back then.

Throughout the Ordovician period, the sea levels were some of the highest they had ever been before or since – an unimaginable 220m higher than they are today – and where there was land, it was concentrated together, not spread out like we see today. Even when the major glaciation took effect and much of the land was covered in ice, sea levels were still 140m higher than they are currently. The land would have been almost entirely without any life, with only a few fungi and early plants, such as liverworts and the ancestors of hornworts and mosses, surviving. This was hundreds of millions of years before trees, grasses and flowering plants would evolve on to the scene. Instead, the vast majority of life was found within the shallow seas surrounding the huge land masses.

The extinction hit in two distinct waves of loss and was the first big extinction event to affect animal-based communities. While there were many individual species and groups that would survive this first mass extinction, *Hallucigenia* sadly wouldn't and is an example of how

At the end of the Ordovician, most of the planet was covered by the superocean Panthalassa. Much of the land was towards the South Pole, with the supercontinent Gondwana being the largest land mass.

extinction can very suddenly stop a species or group of species from evolving. We will never know what might have become of *Hallucigenia* and its descendants, but for a time, these quirky little invertebrates would have featured on any prehistoric visit to a rockpool and many other shallow coastal habitats.

Shallow marine habitats, then and now. Late Ordovician reefs teemed with life. Half a billion years ago, you might have seen *Anomalocaris*, *Odaraia*, and, of course, *Hallucigenia*, rather than hammerhead sharks, dolphins, moray eels, turtles and octopus.

Hallucigenia was a very strange marine invertebrate – an armoured worm covered in spines and frills, which inhabited a planet alien to us today. In a time when giant predatory invertebrates lurked in the shallow-water habitats and the early ancestors of humans were still fish, what caused huge ice sheets to cover the planet? And what caused sea levels to drop, leaving many of the shallow marine ecosystems dry and unable to sustain life at a time when really, it had only just got started?

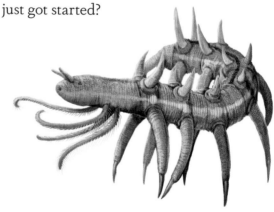

CAUSES 🌡️❄️

When trying to piece together an event that occurred nearly half a billion years ago, it's important to keep an open mind and to remember that there might not be many clues left. First, because of the actions of tectonic plates and the movement of continents, the actual seabed itself gets churned up and almost recycled every 200 million years or so. This means that some evidence, such as a convenient asteroid crater, or fossils themselves are eventually lost.

When looking at the older mass extinctions, there have been some complicated explanations, some strange ideas and, in all honesty, some bonkers theories. An idea that won't go away is related to the End Ordovician event. Some scientists believe that, in a far-off branch of the Milky Way, there was a hypernova, which is a form of huge space explosion, some 6,000 light years from Earth. If one light year is the same distance light can travel over a year, which is about nine trillion km (9,000,000,000,000km), then this particular hypernova would have been approximately 54,000,000,000,000,000km away from where you're sitting now. It would have released a short, but fatal, burst of gamma-ray radiation, which has the smallest wavelengths of any type of energy, so small they can pass between atoms. A ten-second burst would have been all that was needed to strip Earth's atmosphere of half its ozone, a gas which, in high concentrations above the Earth, blocks much of the ultraviolet (UV) energy from hitting the planet. With much of this protective gas suddenly gone, deadly levels of UV radiation would have killed many vulnerable species and groups. This is a cool theory and who doesn't like the idea of a deep space explosion and radiation? Well, evidence-loving scientists, that's who. While what we saw in the End Ordovician event could have been due to gamma radiation, there is no clear evidence that this ever happened and instead, it's a bit of a 'what if' scenario.

Another idea is that there were changes in the actual chemistry of the oceans and that higher levels of arsenic, lead and iron emerging from within the Earth's crust as a result of a long series of raging earthquakes and volcanic eruptions were to blame. These new dangerous levels of minerals and metals – which we know are toxic to life – may have caused strange deformities in the tiny plankton that teemed in Earth's ancient seas nearly 450 million years ago. A possible drop in the ocean oxygen levels may have seen the release of these metals into the ecosystem, destroying food chains from the bottom up.

Rockpools offer shelter to small and delicate organisms. Two *Hallucigenia* share a rockpool with some *Wiwaxia*, which grazed food using their mouth to scrape algae or bacteria.

Another theory suggests that a series of huge volcanic eruptions and dramatic shifts in the tectonic plates in the Earth's crust may have been responsible, by releasing dangerously high levels of carbon dioxide into the atmosphere. Carbon dioxide is essential in our atmosphere, as it helps trap some heat and keeps the planet nice and warm, just right for life to thrive. Too much carbon dioxide, though, means more heat is trapped, which eventually causes the planet to overheat, making it much harder for species to survive.

It's a good idea and we know this does happen (it's starting to happen now). But when we look at the evidence, we can see that just before this first mass extinction, instead of increasing, the level of carbon dioxide around the world had actually dropped by nearly two-thirds.

The truth is that the End Ordovician may have been linked to several of these factors (although not the fatal space gamma-ray theory) and although none of them caused the extinctions directly, they may have contributed towards both. We know there was a sudden cooling of the Earth and that massive glacial ice sheets formed. Unusually, this *actually* might have been caused by the lower levels in carbon dioxide caused by intense volcanic activity from within the Earth's crust and huge geological tectonic processes which were occurring at the time.

Because much of the land mass was positioned in the southern hemisphere around where the South Pole is now, a concentrated (and huge) ancient ice age meant that the entire world's oceans were cooled, from the shallowest points to the deepest parts where life could exist.

With that much ice forming suddenly, the water needed to make it had to come from somewhere. So, in addition to colder oceans, there was suddenly less water *in* those oceans, and this was another major problem of the End Ordovician mass extinction. Shallow habitats around the giant continental land mass not only became cooler but also dried up.

Marine environments were full of life, but the same could not be said on land. The first plants needed to be near water to survive, meaning millions of square kilometres of land would have been lifeless.

There may have been asteroid strikes or deadly metal poisoning, or even catastrophic algal blooms which released toxic chemicals and starved the environments of oxygen, but these things would only have added to the destruction already being caused. When much of the life had adapted to warm, shallow seas, the last thing it needed was a cold environment with no shallow habitats left.

This early global ice age did not last for long. The rapid cooling and sea level drop was only the first phase and this global glacial event ended suddenly. Now, those shallow-water species which had already had to adapt to deeper habitats because of the ice age and lower sea levels had to adapt all over again. When the world warmed, the ice melted and sea levels rose once more. When the sea levels rose too quickly, extra water massively disrupted ocean currents. This might not sound like a serious thing but if currents are disrupted or, worse, break down, then weather patterns collapse and climates change. A combination of the flooding effects of this meltwater and then the impact of major changes in the oceans was too much for many species. They were not able to adapt quickly enough and because they were not suited to rapid and drastic change, or to the new environment in which they found themselves, hundreds of thousands, maybe even millions, of species went extinct.

EFFECTS

As far as mass extinctions went, there was bad news and good news in the End Ordovician. Importantly, as well as losing an estimated 85 per cent of species, it meant a loss of approximately 50 per cent of animal groups, which would have affected the diversity of life and have caused food chains and ecosystems to collapse. While this was obviously a terrible thing, the good news is that no major animal group was lost. There were lots of groups which did make it through this global catastrophe. The trilobites survived, although they lost important members. The echinoderms (which now includes starfish, urchins and sea cucumbers) made it, along with the crinoids (the sea lilies and feather stars). The molluscs, which include snails, sea slugs and cephalopods – now octopuses, squid and cuttlefish – but then included groups such as *Orthoceras*, also succeeded.

Some extinct species resemble those alive today but it's often difficult to tell whether they are actually related. The predatory *Nectocaris* looked like an early relative of squid, and maybe it was, but we are still uncertain.

Most importantly for us, the very early fish representatives made it through this extinction. Jawed fish had only recently evolved and although they looked very different from the fish we might recognise today, we should be thankful these early vertebrates did live, because they would evolve and diversify into all the other vertebrates, including ourselves.

The End Ordovician was marked by the appearance of huge glaciers and falling sea levels worldwide, at a time when much of the planet's land was bunched together near the South Pole. This meant there were lots of very shallow marine ecosystems, which had been perfect for encouraging biodiversity and varied ecosystems. With high levels of light coming in, early corals and algae

were able to turn that light radiation from the sun into energy which could then be used to live and grow, via photosynthesis, and produce energy in these shallow habitats. This meant that complex food chains could develop and that there would have been enough resources to allow lots of producers, herbivores and carnivores, a bit like the busy, bustling coral reefs and rocky shorelines we see today.

When the sea levels dropped suddenly, these shallow coastal habitats literally dried up, leaving species with nowhere to go. Those animals that physically couldn't move perished because suddenly they would have been exposed, out of the water.

In terms of actual numbers of how many species and how many individual organisms were lost, we simply don't know. This is partly because very few dead organisms actually get fossilised and because we are talking about a time so far back in the Earth's history, that we are lucky to know anything, let alone specific details. Overall, fewer shallow marine habitats were left, meaning there would have been fewer places for these shallow water-adapted species to live and where there was opportunity, competition would have been fierce.

The End Ordovician mass extinction was marked by a period of major glaciation, when much of the land was covered by hundreds of metres of ice. Here, the body of a *Hurdia* lies next to a dead *Hallucigenia*.

Also, worldwide glaciation meant worldwide cooling, which was the second major factor in driving the mass extinction. If the lack of habitat didn't kill a species, the colder environment would have. Before the mass extinction, the average temperature across the planet was a couple of degrees warmer than it is today but, as we also see currently, there would have been a lot of variation and some regions were warmer and tropical in terms of their ecosystems. We can still see evidence of this ancient glaciation event in the most unexpected of places – the Sahara desert, where sediment deposits show a clear period where ice sheets would have covered much of the land around 443 million years ago, stretching from what is now northern Africa to the southern end of South America. This vast ice sheet may have been as much as twice the size of Antarctica today and in places, nearly a kilometre thick.

Throughout the End Ordovician, animals living on or near the surface and those in shallower habitats were affected more severely than those living on the seabed or those living in deeper waters, and many would have perished. The extinction came in two stages. The first phase had a big impact but only on a limited number of species, such as those which were physically stuck to one spot and couldn't move, or those which were not able to cope with changes in the environment. In the second part of the End Ordovician extinction, around a million years later, the impact appears to have been more random and more widespread, which resulted in more species being lost.

This second phase of the extinction changed the environments so much on Earth that it marked the end of the Ordovician period and the start of the Silurian (Si lure-EE-an). Life on Earth took several million years to recover from the End Ordovician event, but when it did, many of the new groups and species found themselves in similar ecological niches and habitats. This meant that although this first mass extinction did have a wide-reaching global impact and was the end for many species and groups, such as *Hallucigenia*, it did not have a significant long-term effect.

As Earth recovered and entered the Silurian and then the Devonian (Devv-o nee-an) period, life diversified and changes took place, including the evolution and expansion of one of the most successful groups of vertebrates ever, the fish.

The ecology of the Ordovician marine environment showing carnivores (such as *Anomalocaris*), herbivores and scavengers. Some species actively went looking for their food, while others were filter feeders.

Dr Duncan Murdock is a Research Fellow at the Oxford University Museum of Natural History. He is a palaeontologist studying fossils of some of the earliest animals, especially the first to build skeletons. He looks at how they lived, what modern animals they are related to, and how they came to become fossils.

So, what were the first animals like?

It may seem strange to think about it, but there was a time in the past when there were no animals on Earth. For billions of years, when it came to life, things didn't get more complex than something like a slime mould. Then around 570 million years ago, things started to change and by the time of *Hallucigenia*, all the big groups of animals had arrived on the scene, swimming, scuttling and digging in the mud to change the world forever.

So, what happened in this narrow window of time, and what were the first animals like? We need to look at the fossil record. Large fossils of animals, such as trilobites, can be found in seabed rocks from around 521 million years ago, and before these there are tiny fragments of shells and spines as well as scratches and burrows that are definitely made by animals. These take us to the start of a period known as the Cambrian, about 541 million years ago, when animals not unlike some we see today must have lived – worms with muscles, nerves, a mouth and gut, leaving their tell-tale traces as they search for food in the seafloor mud.

If we delve deeper in time to before the Cambrian, things start to get much weirder. Here, we enter 'tube world', where the first animals with skeletons evolved, growing hard tubes and cup-like structures to live in and creating the world's first reefs, but on a tiny scale. Although what the inhabitants of these tubes looked like is unknown, most scientists agree they were some kind of animal, perhaps something like the corals that live today.

Even further back in time, we find strange, soft-bodied organisms that at first glance bear little resemblance to living animals, but new discoveries are hinting that they might be animals too. Looking a bit like a thumbprint in wet sand, *Dickinsonia* had no mouth or guts, or virtually anything recognisable. But it seems to have been able to move by itself, leaving trail 'footprints', and some fossils of *Dickinsonia* bear a chemical trace that has been suggested to be distinctly animal.

The oldest of all, however, are the rangeomorphs, such as *Charnia*, around 570 million years old. Although they look a little like fronds of a fern, they lived in water too deep for light to penetrate. Once believed to be an entirely extinct 'failed experiment', new evidence suggests they grew in a way that only animals do.

So, what were the first animals like? The answer is that we don't know for sure, but these fossils provide exciting clues. They were almost certainly entirely soft-bodied, living on the seafloor sometime before the Cambrian. They may have been flat discs or fronds, stuck in one place or moving above the mud, or perhaps something stranger still.

HALLUCIGENIA

SOME THINGS are hard to explain, unless you have all the evidence in front of you. Imagine if I asked you and three friends to help me with a rather strange experiment. I need the four of you to stand in a dark room, one in each corner. You can't see anything, and you have to remain silent. I've hidden a friendly elephant (yes, I know this is *may* not be a good idea) in front of you, in the dark, but you can't see it. Each of you is to step forward with your hands raised. You have five seconds to feel around in the dark and touch whatever is in front of you.

One of you feels along the long, swaying trunk. One wraps their arms around a huge tree trunk leg. One touches a large, thin flapping ear, which is partly covered by fuzzy short hair. One of you can feel the low-hanging belly, which is heavy and rumbling. Imagine if you all then left the room and had to explain what was in the room. Would any of you have a good idea about what was standing there? You might have a sneaky suspicion if you felt a tusk, but if each of you only experienced a small part of this friendly elephant, then it would be quite confusing when you got together and described your mystery animal. Just think how much harder it would be if this was the first time anyone had ever encountered an elephant.

DISCOVERY

If you only have a few of the clues, then it can be difficult to interpret the limited information you have before you, and this was what happened with *Hallucigenia* (Ha-LOO-SEE-GEN-ee-a), one of the oldest, most mysterious and downright weirdest animals, ever described. The very strange *Hallucigenia* was discovered in 1911 by the American palaeontologist Charles Doolittle Walcott. Although he was right when he described *Hallucigenia* as a very, very old species of aquatic worm, he was wrong

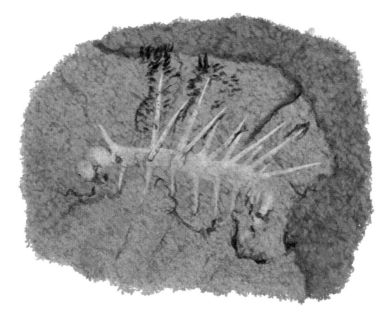

Despite being nearly half a billion years old, some remarkably well-preserved fossils recovered from the Burgess Shale show *Hallucigenia*'s hard spines and soft body parts.

when he thought it was another fossil from a worm that had already been described, called *Canadia*. This used to happen more than you might expect in palaeontology. There was a lot of competition to name new species; frequently, the fossils were fragments; and the technology wasn't anywhere near as good as the scanners and microscopes we have today. Mistakes were made.

Thankfully, scientists who study prehistoric life now have more fossils, better technology and work together to understand the history of life on Earth. Even if we only have a few fossils or even just fragments of fossils, we are able to interpret a mind-blowing amount of detail from them. With better training, huge leaps in technology and more accurate study techniques, scientists are even able to take the fossilised imprint of an eye or a tiny preserved spine and recreate a prehistoric worm that lived half a billion years ago. In many ways, being a scientist is like being a detective, and by understanding science we are able to explore the fascinating, most interesting story in the universe.

At one point, we thought that *Hallucigenia* might be a part of a larger animal. We weren't entirely sure what this animal might have been, but these misidentifications did also sometimes happen. In a similar example, another Cambrian animal called *Anomalocaris* was first identified as being part of a small shrimp, until other body parts were pieced together, and scientists realised that it was a complete animal itself.

ANATOMY

If you and I were chatting about *Hallucigenia* and I tried to describe it to you , our conversation might go something like this:

Me: 'So, there was this really old animal, called *Hallucigenia*.'

You: 'That's a cool name, what did it look like?'

Me: 'Well, it looked almost exactly like a small worm, but... with a head and teeth.'

You: 'A worm with teeth?'

Me: 'And spines, too.'

You: 'What? Are you sure it's a...'

Me: 'Oh, and legs. Did I mention legs?'

You: 'That's not a worm I've ever seen, but it's weird, whatever it is.'

Although you may often hear *Hallucigenia* referred to as being an ancient worm, it was definitely not the sort of worm like those in your garden. Although it may have shared some similarities with

x10 MAGNIFICATION

63cm

> If you saw a living *Hallucigenia*, it would have been small, probably only around half the length of your thumb at most, maybe smaller. Around the time when *Hallucigenia* was alive, there were very few large animals on the planet.

a worm, if you mixed a worm with a caterpillar and a few underwater species (and added a bit of your own imagination), then you're getting closer to understanding how *Hallucigenia* looked. Fossils of *Hallucigenia* show it was a long, thin animal, 5–35mm in length (which is about as long as the word '*Hallucigenia*' on this page). Its legs were arranged in pairs underneath the body and while some had seven pairs, others had eight pairs. Whether they had 14 or 16 legs, at the end of each was a small pair of sharp claws.

Above each set of legs, on the upper side of the body, was a corresponding pair of spines. Rounded at the base and ending in a sharp point, these hard, slender cones were most likely used as a means of defence, as few predators like the idea of a prickly meal which might become stuck in their throat. Not long after the discovery of *Hallucigenia*,

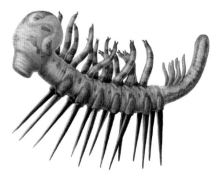

Reconstructing extinct species can be difficult, especially when only pieces of fossils are found or the organism was very small. When *Hallucigenia* was first discovered, palaeontologists accidentally added pieces from other fossilised species to it, until they discovered what it actually looked like.

it was clear there were at least two different species, as the head and spines differed in each. The first to be discovered (*Hallucigenia sparsa*), had a long, thin head and the seven pairs of spines running down its back were long and thin. The second species (*Hallucigenia fortis*) had a big, round head and short, cone-like spines.

More recently, in 2012, a third species (*Hallucigenia hongmeia*) was found and described. It was the largest of the three species, reaching a whopping 35mm in length. It also had short, cone-like spines. But unlike the previous two species, these spines were covered in microscopically small round holes, which palaeontologists believe may have been the points where countless tiny, finger-like structures called papillae (pap-ill-ee) sat, either helping *Hallucigenia* to exchange gases underwater to breathe, or maybe even to 'taste' the environment. The peculiar waving structures, which look like tentacles at the head end of the body, were covered in fine, hair-like material, which we think allowed

Hallucigenia to filter feed. It may even have waved them through the water to trap zooplankton or tiny animals and plants for food. Some fossils have been preserved so well that there is evidence of what the gut may have looked like, although scientists have not yet officially described the insides of this unusual ancient marine organism.

Astonishingly, it took almost 50 years for scientists to fully identify and agree which was the head end and which was the back end of a *Hallucigenia* fossil. One end does stretch out from where the legs and spines are, meaning it would have been able to reach down to the seabed to feed. It was eventually decided that this end would have been the head, and it was only after this discovery was made that other fossils were found where the detail was so good that palaeontologists were able to identify two simple eyes, a mouth lined with teeth and even specialised extra 'teeth' extending towards the gut. These may have meant that *Hallucigenia* was able to chew up its food, helping more effective and efficient digestion.

Understanding the anatomy is only half the story in understanding extinct species; the behaviour is just as important but often more difficult to reveal. Was *Hallucigenia* a predator, scavenger or did it filter food? Was it territorial and if so, did *Hallucigenia* display to one another?

Scientists believe that when *Hallucigenia* fossils are found in the same area, there are sometimes larger, fatter ones and smaller, more slender ones. They think it's possible that these differences might mean the fossils come from males and females, although at the moment, we're not entirely sure which would be the big ones and which would be the smaller ones.

CLASSIFICATION

If I asked you to think about three impressive types of animals, which would you choose? Maybe a whale, some of which have a tongue larger than a car; or birds, which include some that fly between the North and South poles each year, in an endless chase for the best food and breeding grounds; or maybe butterflies, their shimmering wings dazzling us as they fly through our gardens. Emerging from cocoons after spending their early life as pudgy caterpillars, they reorganise every part of their body to make those bright, delicate wings.

I bet you didn't think of a worm, did you? While worms are amazing animals, they don't look especially impressive and they don't really act in a way that makes them memorable when you think about all the other options in the animal kingdom. However, not all worms are the same... some are weirder than others.

And, to confuse things, just because something is *called* a worm, it doesn't mean it has to actually *be* a worm. This can be a peculiarity in biology – the name given to an animal isn't always very accurate. Think about the following three examples. What do you think a frogmouth might be? A frog, right? Nope. Maybe a fish with a big mouth? Wrong. It's a bird. What about a sarcastic fringe head? Maybe a cheeky lizard? Not even close. It's actually a fish which can open its mouth and display the

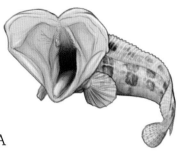

bright, colourful interior in such an extreme way, that you wouldn't believe me if I tried to describe how this unusual example of aquatic territorial behaviour actually works. A mountain chicken is easy, by comparison, surely? It's a bird that lives up a hill and probably lays eggs most days? A mountain chicken is, in fact, a type of large frog that lives on a Caribbean island. The worm called *Hallucigenia* is similar because the name doesn't really tell us much about the worm and, in fact, when we start to look at it, *Hallucigenia* is not even close to being a true worm.

Identifying any new species or animal group is always really exciting and important, but it's equally important to know where this new discovery sits within a larger family tree. This is called taxonomy and although it can be a rather challenging but interesting area of science, you do taxonomy all the time. Next time you walk into a supermarket, you'll do it and probably won't even think about it. You'll see the fresh fruit and vegetables and they will be placed together in groups, based on their similarities or differences. This is exactly the same process we use in scientific classification. In the supermarket example, potatoes and carrots and other vegetables will be together, and apples, oranges, pears and other fruit will sit side by side. You won't need to go looking for carrots between bananas and oranges, because someone will have already sorted the fruit and the vegetables. Then, when you look at apples, for example, different types of apples are near each other – they're not spread over the fresh fruit and vegetable section, are they?

This is what happens with proper scientific taxonomy. Things similar to one another end up close to each other on a family tree, and when lots of species are really similar, then they end up even closer together on the family tree (on the same branch but each taking up an individual twig). The same is done with animals and plants alive today and also for extinct forms of life.

Looking at the classification and family tree of *Hallucigenia*, though, is not easy. It's like being given a 1,000-piece jigsaw and realising there are only 50 pieces of the puzzle inside when you lift the lid. It's going to be pretty hard to put the jigsaw together and you are only ever going to understand a small piece of the overall picture. It's like this for *Hallucigenia*. We only have about 100 different fossil finds for *Hallucigenia* and not all are complete fossils, yet this is what's so interesting about animals which lived around 450 million years ago. We don't have much evidence to go on and it's amazing scientists are able to discover anything at all, but if we want to understand early life and the ecosystems in which they thrived, then we need to use every clue we have.

So, what was *Hallucigenia* and where did it sit within the vast and complex animal kingdom 450 million years ago? It looks like a cross between a worm (with its long, soft body) and an arthropod (with the long-clawed legs of something like an ant or a centipede). In fact, it was neither an arthropod, nor a worm, but belonged to a different fascinating group of animals.

We still don't know absolutely what *Hallucigenia* was most closely related to. Some scientists believe it was an early type of velvet worm (which aren't worms either) or that it fitted somewhere within a bigger group of Panarthropoda (pan-arth RO po-da) animals which included: Onychophora (On-ee coff-orra) the 'velvet worms', Arthropoda (arrth-RO po-da) the 'jointed-legged' invertebrates, and Tardigrada (Tar-DEE gra-da) the 'water bears', all of which are distantly related to each another.

To be a part of the group Panarthropoda, an animal needs to have legs and claws, must have a body made up from segments and must have a nervous system which runs through its body.

When we look at these three very interesting, related groups, we can see that *Hallucigenia* shared some of its body with one group and some with the other groups. The panarthropods are astounding and, in a few cases, a bit bonkers. Some of these animals are among the most familiar, the most interesting and the toughest organisms on the planet. When we look at the panarthropods, it's pretty clear that despite sharing some similarities, these animals are different in many ways. This makes the panarthropods (including *Hallucigenia*) of huge palaeontological interest, as they can help us reconstruct the lives of prehistoric invertebrates and understand how the whole group evolved.

Velvet worms (or onychophorans)

These little-known animals are referred to as velvet worms because they look like worms and as though they are covered in velvet. But they are not covered in velvet and, in fact, are not even worms. The scientific name for their group is Onychophora, which comes from two ancient Greek words which mean 'claws' and 'to carry', but they are also known as peripatus (per-ipp at-tus). Velvet worms are long, soft-bodied panarthropods, which have lots of legs. Although they look like worms, caterpillars or even slugs, they're not, but are a different, stand-alone group. Around 200 species of velvet worms have been scientifically described, but it is thought that many more species are waiting to be discovered. There are two main groups of velvet worms: one is found mainly in tropical areas around the equator and the other to the south of the equator.

Velvet worms vary massively in size and while some are only half a centimetre long, others are up to 20cm. They prey on smaller animals within their environment and have a special way of hunting. When they target potential prey, they squirt out a sticky, slime-like substance which coats their victims and hardens on contact. The velvet worm then injects digestive juices into its trapped prey before eating the partly dissolved meal.

Water bears (or tardigrades)

There's always been the idea that at the end of the world after some global disaster, there would be just cockroaches left, as they have the reputation for being the toughest animals on the planet. But move over cockroaches, because the water bears are in town. Fondly called water bears because they appear to resemble lumbering, fat-bodied little bears which are often found in or near water, these animals are usually around 0.5mm in length and are known scientifically as tardigrades (tar-DEE grades), which means 'slow walker'. They are plump, eight-legged animals (with claws or suckers on their feet), which have segmented bodies and live in or near to water. And they are tough.

Tardigrades can be found almost everywhere, from the tops of the highest mountains to the bottom of the deepest parts of the oceans. They live in tropical rain forests and in the frozen habitats of the South Pole. They seem to thrive in extreme conditions, and if conditions are too extreme, then they can enter what seems to be a state of suspended animation. To see just how tough they are, scientists have tested them to the limits of what's possible. They can survive temperatures as low as -200°C and almost as high as 150°C. In fact, extreme radiation, boiling liquids and pressure six times greater than the deepest oceans present no problems for the tardigrades. In 2019, when a lunar spacecraft crash-landed on the moon, it was reported that a container full of tardigrades had been on board. We may never know for sure, but there could be a colony of little space tardigrades alive on the moon.

Arthropods

This is a huge group and although there may be a couple of species you might not be fully aware of, they are quite

possibly the most important group of animals on the planet. Meaning 'jointed foot', an arthropod is an invertebrate which possesses an external skeleton (an exoskeleton), has a segmented body and pairs of legs. The group includes all the insects, arachnids and crustaceans. So far, over one and a half million species of arthropods have been described by scientists, representing over 80 per cent of all known living species on Earth. Some scientists believe, however, that there may be as many as another 10 million species of arthropod which haven't yet been discovered and described – which is maybe five times the number of all species of life so far described.

Their skeletons, on the outside of their body, are made from a hard substance called chitin. They cannot grow in the same way that we can. Instead, they shed their exoskeletons throughout their life, which enables them to grow larger each time. Some arthropods are carnivores, some are herbivores, and some are omnivores. Some have wings, some don't. Some have six legs, some have many more. Arthropods range greatly in size, from the Japanese spider crabs, which have a leg span up to 4m across, to microscopic marine invertebrates which are about ten times smaller than this full stop. Because they are so varied in terms of their size, shape and behaviour, arthropods are incredibly successful and can be found in almost every habitat on the planet.

What was *Hallucigenia*?

So, what really was *Hallucigenia* and how did it fit in with these other animals? Our best understanding is that *Hallucigenia* was probably an early member of the group Panarthropoda, and is an extinct relative of the tardigrades, arthropods and velvet worms. They are often referred to as being lobopodian (lob-O PO DEE-an) worms, which were ancient, worm-like animals with stubby feet and belonged within the Panarthropoda.

How all these relationships work, and which animals are most closely related to *Hallucigenia*, is still the subject of debate and research but the more we understand about

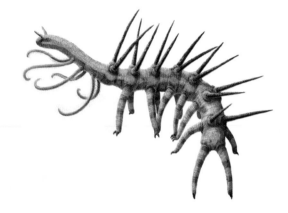

Hallucigenia, the more we shall understand about some of the most fascinating, successful and diverse animals alive today. The important thing to remember is that although it may have looked like a worm, it was not a worm, but an animal which gives us an insight into one of the earliest and most important points in the evolutionary journey of life on Earth.

Only 109 different fossils for *Hallucigenia* have been found up to now. While *Hallucigenia sparsa* seems to have had a global distribution, so far both *Hallucigenia fortis* and *Hallucigenia hongmeia* have only been found in what is now China.

Two large *Hallucigenia* displaying to one another at a rich feeding spot on the reef.

ECOLOGY 🦐

By looking at the ecology of a species, we get a more complete picture of how the animal lives (or lived) and which factors influence its evolution. By ecology, we mean how an animal, plant, fungi or other group of organisms lives, where it lives and the role it plays within its environment.

The ecology of some species is clear. The basking shark, for example, is the second largest fish in the world. It is a filter feeder and travels thousands of kilometres each year in search of food and breeding grounds. We know what it eats, which animals pluck parasites from it, how big it gets, how fast it swims, and we even know when the basking sharks arrive in UK waters each year, as they feed along the western coast of the British Isles. However, even with these giant animals, there is still so much we don't know about them. We know very little about their reproduction, what life is like for young basking sharks, or even where the adults spend much of the year.

Imagine how much harder (yet rewarding) it is to understand the ecology of a small organism, which was only 2-3cm long and lived half a billion years ago, from just a hundred or so fossils. That's the situation not only with *Hallucigenia* but also with any organism from this time period. To understand its ecology, we need high-tech equipment and techniques, as many fossils as possible, good scientists and a slice of luck.

For all the uncertainties surrounding *Hallucigenia*, we can be sure it lived in a world very different to the one we know today. If you travelled back over 500 million years, the planet and the animals which inhabited it would have looked completely alien to us. Many people say that the Earth today is a 'blue planet', as more than 70 per cent of it is covered by oceans. During the Cambrian period, however, which stretched from 541 million years ago to 485.4 million years ago, it would have looked even more like a watery world, as we believe that nearly all the land was in the southern hemisphere, forming a supercontinent called Pannotia (pan-no-TEE-a).

Strange as it may seem, however, we are not certain yet whether Pannotia did actually exist or not. If it *did* exist, it is thought that this supersized land mass broke up throughout the Cambrian period.

By the time *Hallucigenia* was wandering around, tectonic activity, caused by the movement of the huge plates mostly within the Earth's crust, was already forcing Pannotia to separate and move very slowly northwards, where it would (some scientists think) go on to form the more well-known supercontinent Pangaea (pan JEE-a).

When

The best preserved *Hallucigenia* fossils appear to date back to around 505 million years ago.

Where

Fossils from *Hallucigenia* are found in two main locations: in the Burgess Shale in British Columbia, Canada; and in the Maotianshan Shale, in China. Not all three species are found in the same places, though. The most widespread was *Hallucigenia sparsa*, which seems to have had a worldwide distribution, whereas fossils from both *Hallucigenia fortis* and *Hallucigenia hongmeia* have so far only been found in what is now China.

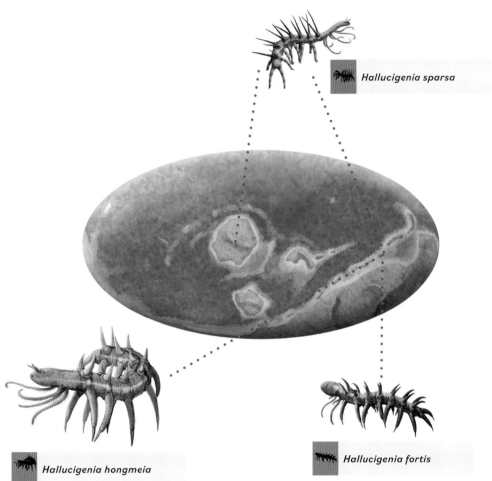

Hallucigenia sparsa

Hallucigenia hongmeia

Hallucigenia fortis

This is how the Earth looked in the End Ordovician period. So far, three species of *Hallucigenia* have been identified by palaeontologists. Their fossils are found in what is now North America and China.

Environment

Our best understanding of what life was like towards the end of the Cambrian comes from looking at a place called the Burgess Shale. This incredible fossil bed was discovered in 1909 by Charles Doolittle Walcott (who would later find the first fossils of *Hallucigenia*). Not only was it bursting with a huge number of fossils, but these fossils were special. Quite unusually, they showed amazing detail as the soft parts of the animals had been preserved, rather than just the hard exoskeleton, scales or bones. The Burgess Shale is in the middle of the Rockies mountain range in British Columbia, Canada. It dates back to 508 million years ago and is one of the oldest sites showing soft body fossils from anywhere in the world. It gives us an idea of what life was really like half a billion years ago, when most animals did not have any hard body parts which could more easily be preserved in the fossil record.

Imagine if I visited your home but could not see anything soft. I would not see any clothes, carpets or bed sheets. Even your sofas would look like wooden frames with uncomfortable springs poking out. To get a complete understanding of where you live, I would need to see the soft and hard objects in your home. It's the same with any environment, either now or from a point in prehistory, long ago.

Flora and fauna

If you had waded into the warm shallow waters of the Cambrian marine habitat, put on a mask and gone for a snorkel, to look for a living *Hallucigenia*, you'd have been amazed at how much life there was and how unusual it would have looked. None of the animals looked like anything alive today.

Most of the animals living alongside *Hallucigenia* could be said to be bottom dwelling within these shallower coastal environments. They would either have been physically attached to the seabed or weren't able to move too far away from it. *Hallucigenia* was one of these 'benthic' animals, as it was always found on the bottom part of its environment. In terms of competition, *Hallucigenia* would have been one of many animals (maybe as much as a third) that filtered food from the

A huge decomposing *Anomalocaris* provides a meal for two trilobites, some *Naraoia* and lots of *Hallucigenia*, filtering planktonic food from the current.

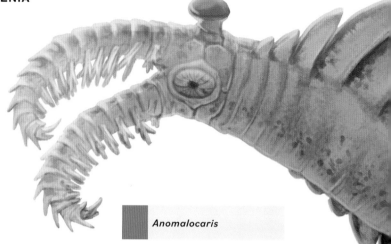

Anomalocaris

water in order to feed. Most, such as the bristly *Wiwaxia* and *Ottoia* with its hook-lined proboscis, fed in the muddy seabed, but around 10 per cent were predators. These included the arthropod *Opabinia* with its bizarre claw, or *Anomalocaris*, the fearsome, armoured, shrimp-like, trilobite-eating 'superpredator' of these early marine environments, both of which actively hunted their next meals. At the time, *Anomalocaris* may have been one of the largest organisms on the planet, measuring an impressive 1m in length.

Wiwaxia

Opabinia

If it hadn't been armed with defensive spines, a soft-bodied animal like *Hallucigenia* would have been on the menu for many different animals, like *Opabinia*.

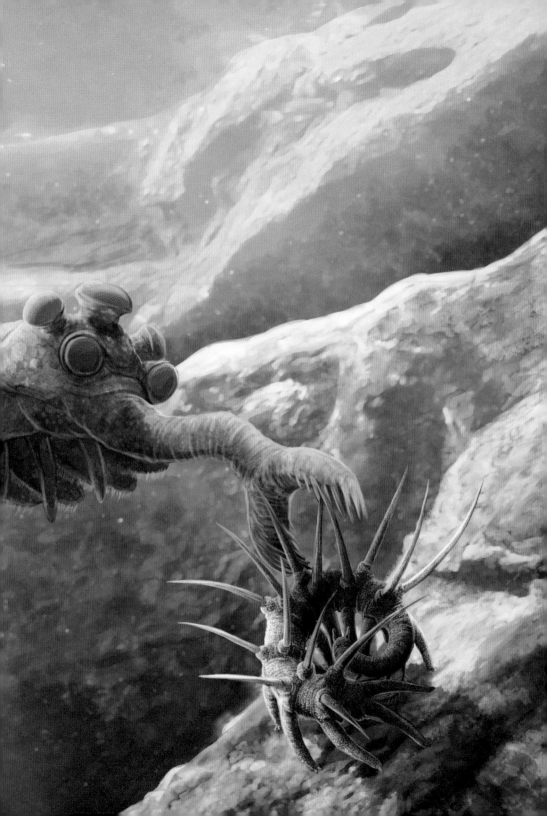

Behaviour 🐟🐟🐟

Looking at *Hallucigenia*'s mouth, specialised 'teeth' and little 'arms' adapted for filter feeding, it is likely it was a detritivore (DEE TRY-TI vor), which means it ate dead and rotting material, rather than actively hunting. For a long time, scientists had *Hallucigenia* the wrong way up, imagining the spines were in contact with the seabed (or corals or sponges). This would have been a rubbish way of getting around in terms of energy use, or might have meant they used their spines to dig into the habitat to anchor themselves. We now know the sharp spines run along what is the top of the body and the short tentacles are legs, which it could have used to move around its environment. This makes a lot more sense because, like this, the spines are used for defence and the tentacle-like structures would function well as legs.

But, as with almost everything about *Hallucigenia*, there is still much we are unsure about. It is not possible to see on the fossils whether the tentacles are paired or not, as you might expect with the legs. Some researchers do not think the spines were hard, because they have, so far, not been found on their own, as you might expect when a soft-bodied animal with some hard parts dies (think about snail shells).

As far as defensive weapons go, the spines covered the main part of the body, leaving the front and back ends unguarded. Did *Hallucigenia* have extra defences we don't know about? Did they burrow under the sand, or into the body of a sponge, with just their head and filter-feeding parts, as well as their body spines, exposed? Did they curl up into a defensive ball, tucking their head and tail under the protection of their spines, until a predator passed? As you might expect with a small, soft-bodied animal living half a billion years ago, reconstructing its life might be great fun but it's also practically impossible.

GLOSSARY

Arthropod (AR-throw pod)
An invertebrate animal with an exoskeleton and segmented pairs of legs. Insects, such as ants; arachnids, such as spiders; and crustaceans, such as crabs, are all examples of arthropods.

Benthic
The lowest level of an aquatic ecosystem. It might be a stream bed and the water just above it, or the bottom of the ocean, with the seabed and water just above it being the benthic zone.

Biodiversity (BI-O DIE-vers it-EE)
The variety of plants, fungi, animals and other groups of organisms within a particular habitat or ecosystem. A healthy habitat or ecosystem will usually have higher levels of biodiversity.

Carbon dioxide
A naturally occurring greenhouse gas. At normal levels, carbon dioxide is essential for trapping some levels of heat

energy within our environment. When levels get too high, overheating occurs.

Chitin (Kii-tin)
A strong but flexible substance found in the exoskeletons of arthropods.

Chytrid (kit-rid)
A fungal disease which affects frogs and other amphibians. The full name for the disease is chytridiomycosis (kit-rid EE-o MY-co-sis).

Crustaceans (crus-TAY shuns)
A large group of aquatic organisms within the arthropods. Most crustaceans are found within a marine environment. Examples include crabs, lobsters, shrimps, krill and barnacles.

Detritivore (DEE TRY-TI vor)
An organism which mainly eats rotting plant material. Earthworms and dung beetles are examples of detritivores.

Ecology
The particular area of biology where the focus is on the relationship between organisms and their physical surroundings.

Ecosystem
The community of organisms (animals, plants and other major groups) and their physical environment.

Endothermic (en-DOW thur-mik)
The ability of an animal to create its own body heat through internal bodily processes. Often, the phrase 'warm blooded' is used but this is not as accurate as 'endothermic'.

Exoskeleton
A rigid external covering for the body in some invertebrate animals, especially arthropods such as insects and crustaceans.

Gamma ray
A type of radiation that has the smallest wavelengths of any type of energy. The wavelengths are so small they can pass between atoms. Gamma-ray radiation is lethal.

Genetics
The study of how features are passed on from one generation to the next, such as hair colour, stripes or size.

Hybridisation
The process by which an animal, plant, etc. breeds with an individual of another species or subspecies.

Hypernova
The largest type of space explosion. A star exploding is an example of a hypernova.

Invertebrate
Any animal which does not have (and will never have) backbones, or vertebrae.

Light year
The same distance light can travel over a year, which is the same as about nine trillion km.

Lobopodian (lob-O PO DEE-an)
A group of extinct worm-like animals, with stubby legs. The name means 'blunt feet'.

Niche (NEE-shh)
The match of an organism to a specific environmental condition. The ecological niche takes into account food, any possible predators and prey, the habitat, etc.

Onychophora (On-ee coff-orra)
Part of the Panarthropoda group of animals, known also as velvet worms. These animals are still alive today.

Organism (or-gan IZ-mm)
Any living thing. A tree is an organism, so is a shark, and a mushroom. *You* are an organism.

Ozone
A gas naturally found in high concentrations above the Earth. Ozone blocks much of the ultraviolet (UV) energy from the sun from hitting the planet.

Panarthropoda (pan-arth RO po-da)
A group of animals that includes tardigrades, velvet worms and the lobopodian worms such as *Hallucigenia*. There is some disagreement between scientists whether this is a

proper group of organisms. Some say they are not similar enough to form one related group.

Pangaea (pan JEE-a)
A supercontinent from around 335 million years ago, made up from the modern land masses which back then sat together. Pangaea started to break up through the movement of tectonic plates about 175 million years ago.

Pannotia (pan-no-TEE-a)
A supercontinent from around 650 million years ago, made up from the modern land masses which back then sat together. Pannotia started to break up through the movement of tectonic plates about 560 million years ago and would eventually go on to form Pangaea. There are still some scientists who are not 100 per cent certain that Pannotia actually existed.

Papillae (pap-ill-ee)
These are very small rounded finger-like 'bumps' on an organism, sometimes (but not always) microscopic, and used in a variety of functions such as sensing the environment.

Peripatus (per-ipp at-tus)
Also known as velvet worms, these are technically known as Onychophora. They are part of the Panarthropoda group and are still alive today.

Proboscis
In invertebrates, a proboscis is a straw-like or tube-like sucking mouthpart. In some worms, the proboscis is extendible.

Rangeomorph
An extinct group of organisms which looked like ferns. These are some of the oldest organisms on the planet and might be some of the first examples of animals, although right now, scientists are still not 100 per cent certain they were definitely animals.

Tardigrades (tar-DEE grades)
A group of aquatic or semi-aquatic animals, also known as water bears or moss piglets. They are part of the Panarthropoda group, have eight legs and have been shown to survive very high temperatures such as hot springs and temperatures as low as –272 °C. They have even recently been taken into space.

Taxonomy
The method used to put different organisms into groups based on how similar they are to one another. The taxonomy of fruit and vegetables, for example, might be to put all the different types of berries together and then tomatoes, peppers and cucumbers next to them, because they all have lots of seeds.

Tectonic (tek-ton-ik)
Relating to the structure of the Earth's crust and the processes which occur within it.

Ultraviolet (UV)
A type of energy produced by the sun.

Zooplankton
The tiny animal organisms found in marine and some freshwater ecosystems.

Collect all eight titles
in the  EXTINCT series

 Hallucigenia

 *Dunkleosteus*

 *Trilobite*

 Lisowicia

 *Tyrannosaurus rex*

Megalodon

Thylacine

Hainan gibbon

THE STORY OF LIFE ON EARTH

EXTINCT
HALLUCIGENIA

SUPER-WEIRD

BEN GARROD
ILLUSTRATED BY GABRIEL UGUETO

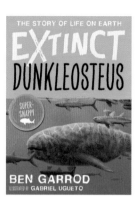

THE STORY OF LIFE ON EARTH

EXTINCT
DUNKLEOSTEUS

SUPER-SNAPPY

BEN GARROD
ILLUSTRATED BY GABRIEL UGUETO

THE STORY OF LIFE ON EARTH

EXTINCT
TRILOBITE

SUPER-INVADERS

BEN GARROD
ILLUSTRATED BY GABRIEL UGUETO

THE STORY OF LIFE ON EARTH

EXTINCT
LISOWICIA

SUPER-SIZED

BEN GARROD
ILLUSTRATED BY GABRIEL UGUETO

THE STORY OF LIFE ON EARTH

EXTINCT
TYRANNOSAURUS REX

SUPER-MISUNDERSTOOD

BEN GARROD
ILLUSTRATED BY GABRIEL UGUETO

THE STORY OF LIFE ON EARTH

EXTINCT
MEGALODON

SUPER-PREDATOR

BEN GARROD
ILLUSTRATED BY GABRIEL UGUETO

THE STORY OF LIFE ON EARTH

EXTINCT
THYLACINE

SUPER-HUNTED

BEN GARROD
ILLUSTRATED BY GABRIEL UGUETO

THE STORY OF LIFE ON EARTH

EXTINCT
HAINAN GIBBON

SUPER-SURVIVOR?

BEN GARROD
ILLUSTRATED BY GABRIEL UGUETO

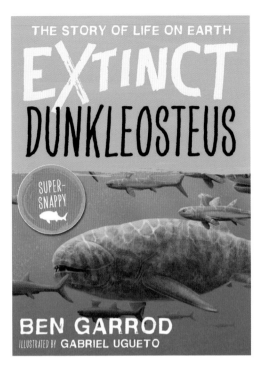

THE STORY OF LIFE ON EARTH

EXTINCT
DUNKLEOSTEUS

SUPER-SNAPPY

BEN GARROD
ILLUSTRATED BY **GABRIEL UGUETO**

An armoured fish with a bite 10 times more powerful than that of a great white shark, *Dunkleosteus* could also snap its jaws five times faster than you can blink! It was one of the most iconic predators ever to rule the waves. What was it like to live in its shadow? And how did it become one of the many victims of the Late Devonian mass extinction around 375 million years ago?

Let's discover why this mass extinction only affected ocean life and why it went on for so long – some scientists believe it lasted for 25 million years. In a weird twist, we'll look at whether the evolution of trees on the land at that time was partly responsible for the loss of so many marine species, including *Dunkleosteus*.

Among the first arthropods - animals with jointed legs such as insects and their relatives - trilobites were around on Earth for over 300 million years and survived the first two mass extinctions. There were once at least 20,000 species but all disappeared in the devastating End Permian mass extinction around 252 million years ago.

We'll look at why land animals were affected this time as well as those in the sea. An incredible 96 per cent of marine species went extinct and an almost equally terrible 70 per cent of life on land was wiped out in what is known as the *Great Dying*. This was the closest we've come to losing all life on Earth and the planet was changed forever.

THE STORY OF LIFE ON EARTH

EXTINCT
LISOWICIA

SUPER-SIZED

BEN GARROD

ILLUSTRATED BY GABRIEL UGUETO

At a massive 9 tonnes, the elephant-sized *Lisowicia* was one of the largest animals on the planet during the Late Triassic. A kind of cross between a mammal and a reptile but not quite either, *Lisowicia* was a distant cousin of the ancient mammals – and they eventually led to our very own ancestors.

We'll discover why the End Triassic mass extinction happened, changing the global environment and making life impossible for around 75 per cent of species. And how, while this fourth mass extinction may have been devastating for most life on Earth, it gave one group of animals – dinosaurs – the chance to dominate the planet for millions of years.

THE STORY OF LIFE ON EARTH

EXTINCT

TYRANNOSAURUS REX

SUPER-MISUNDERSTOOD

BEN GARROD

ILLUSTRATED BY **GABRIEL UGUETO**

Weighing as much as three adult elephants and as long as a bus, *Tyrannosaurus rex* was one of the mightiest land predators that has ever lived. It had the most powerful bite of any dinosaur and dominated its environment. But not even the biggest dinosaurs were a match for what happened at the end of the Cretaceous, about 66 million years ago.

What happened when an asteroid travelling at almost 40,000km/h crashed into Earth? Creating a shockwave that literally shook the world, its impact threw millions of tonnes of red-hot ash and dust into the atmosphere, blocking out the sun and destroying 75 per cent of life on Earth. Any living thing bigger than a fox was gone and this fifth global mass extinction meant the end of the dinosaurs as we knew them.

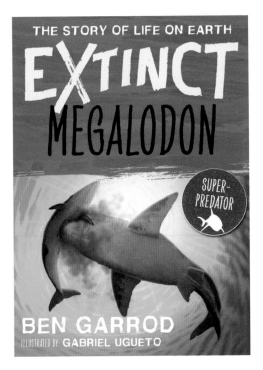

THE STORY OF LIFE ON EARTH

EXTINCT
MEGALODON

SUPER-PREDATOR

BEN GARROD
ILLUSTRATED BY **GABRIEL UGUETO**

A giant marine predator, megalodon grew up to an incredible 18m – longer than three great white sharks, nose to tail. This ferocious monster had the most powerful bite force ever measured. It specialised in killing whales by attacking them from the side, aiming for their heart and lungs.

But, like more than 50 per cent of marine mammals and many others, megalodon disappeared in the End Pliocene mass extinction around 2.5 million years ago. We'll find out why this event affected many of the bigger animals in the marine environment and had an especially bad impact on both warm-blooded animals and predators.

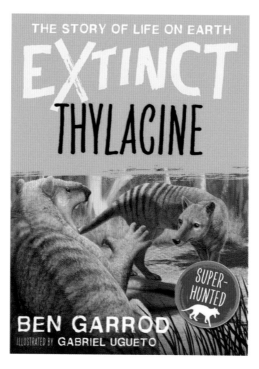

THE STORY OF LIFE ON EARTH

EXTINCT
THYLACINE

SUPER-
HUNTED

BEN GARROD
ILLUSTRATED BY GABRIEL UGUETO

The thylacine, also known as the Tasmanian tiger, is one of a long list of species, ranging from sabre-toothed cats to the dodo, that have been wiped out by humans. The last wild thylacine was shot in 1930 and the last captive thylacine alive died in a zoo in 1936.

We'll explore the mass extinction we are now entering and how we, as a species, have the power to wipe out other species – something no other single species is able to do. Who are the winners and losers and why might it take over seven million years to restore mammal diversity on Earth to what it was before humans arrived?

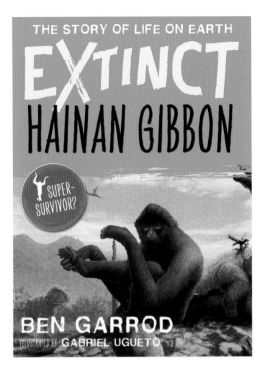

THE STORY OF LIFE ON EARTH

EXTINCT
HAINAN GIBBON

SUPER-SURVIVOR?

BEN GARROD

ILLUSTRATED BY GABRIEL UGUETO

One of the most endangered animals on our planet, the Hainan gibbon is also one of our closest living relatives. Family groups of these little primates live in the trees on an island off the south coast of China and they feed on leaves and fruit.

But the gibbons are now in serious trouble because of the effects of human population increase around the world and habitat destruction. Without action, this animal might soon be extinct and need a dagger after its name. What can we all do to help stop some of our most interesting, iconic and important species from going extinct?

BEN GARROD is Professor of Evolutionary Biology and Science Engagement at the University of East Anglia. Ben has lived and worked all around the world, alongside chimpanzees in Africa, polar bears in the Arctic and giant dinosaur fossils in South America. He is currently based in the West Country. He broadcasts regularly on TV and radio and is trustee and ambassador of a number of key conservation organisations. His debut six-book series *So You Think You Know About... Dinosaurs?* and *The Chimpanzee and Me* are also published by Zephyr.

GABRIEL UGUETO is a scientific illustrator, palaeoartist and herpetologist based in Florida. For several years, he was an independent herpetologist researcher and authored papers on new species of neotropical lizards and various taxonomic revisions. As an illustrator, his work reflects the latest scientific hypotheses about the external appearance and the behaviour of the animals, both extinct and extant, that he reconstructs. His illustrations have appeared in books, journals, magazines, museum exhibitions and television documentaries.

Zephyr is an imprint of Head of Zeus.
At Zephyr we are proud to publish books
you can read and re-read time and time
again because they tell a brilliant story
and because they entertain you.

 @_ZephyrBooks

@_zephyrbooks

HeadofZeusBooks

readzephyr.com

www.headofzeus.com

ZEPHYR